The Heart of Humility

Teaching Kids to Put Others First

By Luke Gilkerson

The Heart of Humility: Teaching Kids to Put Others First

By: Luke Gilkerson
Cover Design: Sarah Thomas

Intoxicated on Life • Copyright 2014 Luke Gilkerson

This workbook is licensed for family use. You may not make copies without the authors written consent. If you would like to purchase your own copy, visit [IntoxicatedOnLife.com](http://intoxicatedonlife.com). All contents copyright 2014 by Luke & Trisha Gilkerson (http://intoxicatedonlife.com). All rights reserved.

This publication is protected under the US Copyright Act of 1976 and all other applicable international, federal, state, and local laws, and all rights are reserved.

TABLE OF CONTENTS

Introduction

How To Use This Study

1. Meet the Philippians
2. Meet Paul
3. The Problem in Philippi: No Unity
4. The Solution: Humility
5. Obstacle to Humility: Selfishness
6. The Fruit of Selfishness: Grumbling and Disputing
7. The Fruit of Humility: Oneness
8. Review: The Importance of Humility

9. Motivation for Humility: Encouragement in Christ
10. Motivation for Humility: Comfort from Love
11. Motivation for Humility: Participation in the Spirit
12. Motivation for Humility: Affection and Sympathy
13. Motivation for Humility: The Joy of Others
14. Review: 5 Motivations for Humility

15. The Example of Humility: Jesus, the One We Worship
16. The Example of Humility: Jesus, the One Who Let Go
17. The Example of Humility: Jesus, the True Man
18. The Example of Humility: Jesus the Servant
19. The Example of Humility: Jesus, Who Obeyed to the End
20. The Example of Humility: Jesus, Who Died for Our Sins
21. The Example of Humility: Jesus, the Exalted One
22. Review: The Example of Christ

23. Motivation for Humility: We are Saved from Sin
24. Motivation for Humility: God is at Work Among Us
25. Motivation for Humility: Pleasing God
26. Motivation for Humility: Being Blameless Witnesses
27. Motivation for Humility: The Word of Life
28. Motivation for Humility: The Day of Christ
29. Motivation for Humility: The Example of Our Teachers
30. Review: 7 More Motivations for Humility

INTRODUCTION

As parents, there are different ways we can help our children understand the Word of God. The first and probably most common way is by giving them a broad understanding of Scripture. By reading through major Bible stories and events, year after year, we give them "the big picture" of the Bible from beginning to end. This is vital for them to develop a Biblical worldview.

Second, we can spend time drilling deep to specific books or passages. We teach our children the value of contemplating a single word or phrase, showing them just how rich the Bible can be. This models for our children the art of studying the Bible in all its fullness and teaches them to pause and reflect all the words God has inspired.

This family devotional is an example of the second way. It will help your children grasp the rich truths contained in Philippians 2:1-18.

HOW TO USE THIS STUDY

There are at least a couple ways you could use this family devotional.

You could spend 30 days in a row, working through one lesson each day. This will immerse your children in the passage.

You could spend 30 weeks doing one lesson each week. You might choose to do this over the duration of one school year.

I would suggest using not one, but both of these approaches, particularly if you will be memorizing this passage of Scripture. Spend 30 days going through this study to acquaint your family with the text prior to memorizing the text. This will help them understand why you are memorizing it. Then, use the Bible study weekly throughout the year to study this Scripture at a slower pace and reinforce the lessons that were already covered once.

Make it a Goal to Memorize

Over the next several months or throughout an entire school year, make a commitment to memorize all of Philippians 2:1-18 as a family.

There is great benefit to memorizing Scripture, and an added benefit to memorizing a lengthier text like this. Memorizing a whole chapter or longer passage gives our children a sense of context. They can begin seeing how to interpret the Bible, seeing how to read a whole section of Scripture in context.

Why Memorize Philippians 2:1-18?

There are many texts in the Bible worth memorizing. Why is Philippians 2:1-18 such a good passage learn?

First, if you're looking for a good passage that marries central Christian beliefs and important Christian ethics, Philippians 2 is great for this. It is hard to find a more compact section of Scripture that equips kids with both foundational beliefs and vital moral lessons.

Second, this passage teaches one of the central pillars of Christians character: humility. Learning what it means to esteem others more important than yourself is a lifelong process. These 18 verses pack in more than a dozen motivations for why we should pursue a life of humility.

Third, the passage contains one of the most concise and rich accounts of Jesus' incarnation, life, death, and exaltation. As we teach our kids what it means to be humble and put others first, as we teach ourselves this, this text helps us to see Jesus as our ultimate example and the one we worship.

For some, 18 verses might sound like a lot, but it takes less than two minutes to read.

Memory Method: Using Scripture Memory Cards

One of the best ways to move Scripture from short-term to long-term memory is to use a Charlotte-Mason-style "memory box."

You'll find free printouts on our site http://intoxicatedonlife.com/freebies/ . There Philippians 2:1-18 is divided into manageable sections (2-3 verses) on individual index cards.

You'll also find printable tabbed dividers to help organize your cards available to download for free on our website http://intoxicatedonlife.com/freebies/. You'll find...

- A tab marked "Daily"
- A tab marked "Odd Days" and another marked "Even Days"
- Weekly tabs (a tab for each day of the week)
- Monthly tabs (tabs numbered 1-30)

Here's how it works:

1. Place all your tabbed dividers into the box in order.
2. Start by placing the first Philippians card behind the "Daily" tab. Review this card with your child daily, having him or her recite it aloud every day.
3. Once your child can quote an entire card from memory with ease, move it back to either the "odd" tab or "even" tab. Then, only review that card on odd or even dates of the month.
4. Once your child continues to quote the card without help for a couple weeks, move it back to one of the weekly tabs.
5. If they can quote the card several weeks in a row without help, then move it back to one of the monthly tabs.
6. As cards move out from behind the daily tab, add new cards to the daily memory time.

Use Handwriting to Teach

In Deuteronomy 17:18-19, the kings of Israel were commanded to write out for themselves a copy of the law of Moses so that they could read it all the days of their lives. God clearly sees value in not only reading the Bible daily, but also in copying the text of the Bible by hand.

A good way to reinforce Scripture memory (and practice handwriting skills) is to copy Bible passages by hand. **As a companion to this Bible study, you can get a copy of our Philippians 2 version of** *Write Through the Bible*, **available at IntoxicatedOnLife.com.**

These workbooks take 135 days to complete, about one school year, and combines the disciplines of handwriting, dictation, vocabulary, and Bible memory into one daily activity. The Write Through the Bible downloadable workbooks are available in both manuscript and cursive and in either KJV or ESV translations.

Praying the "Philippians Prayer" for Your Kids

Nearly anyone can memorize a long text if they are motivated. But only God can use that text to change hearts. This is why we must pray, just as the apostle Paul did, that the truths of this letter will penetrate our children's hearts and develop their character.

As your kids spend a lot of time in Philippians, set aside time each day or each week to pray for your kids the same way Paul prayed for the church in Philippi. In Philippians 1:9-11, Paul told the church how he prayed for them.

"And it is my prayer that your love may abound more and more, with knowledge and all discernment, so that you may approve what is excellent, and so be pure and blameless for the day of Christ, filled with the fruit of righteousness that comes through Jesus Christ, to the glory and praise of God."

Paul prayed for two primary things for his friends in Philippi: (1) that their love would grow deeper and richer, and (2) that their knowledge and discernment would expand. Paul believed if these two things were growing they would become people who could choose not just what is *good*, but what is *best* (or "excellent").

The more the Philippians were motivated by love, the more they would *want* what is best for others and themselves. The more their love was informed by insight and knowledge, the more they would *know* what is best.

As they chose the things that were best, three things would be the result: (1) they would be sincere or pure in their faith as they anticipated the Day of Christ, (2) they would be blameless or without offense, and (3) they would be filled with the fruit of righteousness.

Make this a prayer for your children as they memorize Philippians 2:1-18:

"Lord, I want my children to be sincere, blameless, and righteous as they look forward to the Day of Christ. So, deepen their love and grow their knowledge so they become people who choose what is best in life. Amen."

THE HEART OF HUMILITY
Teaching your children to put others first.

LESSON 1: Meet The Philippians

Opening Thought:

- Have you ever heard of the book of Philippians in the Bible? (*See if your children have heard of it before. Perhaps they have the books of the Bible memorized. If so, see if they can recite the books of the New Testament for you.*)

- Do you know what a Philippian is? (*A Philippian was someone who lived in the old city of Philippi. Show your children a map in your Bible or other book so they can see where Philippi was.*)

We're going to be reading about what happened in the city of Philippi a long time ago.

Scripture Reading: Read Acts 16:16-34

Explanation: Paul was in Philippi telling others about Jesus and some of the people were becoming Christians. But when Paul came to Philippi he encountered problems right away.

Shortly after getting there, he cast an evil spirit out of a slave girl by the power of Jesus. The spirit gave the girl special powers to know things that ordinary people didn't know, and her masters used that power to make lots of money. So when Paul cast the evil spirit out, this made her masters very mad. They had Paul and his friend Silas arrested, beaten up, and thrown in prison.

From that day forward, the new church in Philippi was not going to be very popular. Everyone was going to remember that Christians like Paul have a powerful message. The spirits and the gods the people worshipped in Philippi were no match for the power of Jesus, and Christians taught that only the true God should be worshipped.

The night Paul and Silas were in prison, God caused an earthquake in the city, shaking the prison and made all the prison doors open. That night the prison guard invited Paul and Silas into his home and he and his family became Christians.

We know the church in Philippi went through hard times after Paul left. They were persecuted for their belief in Jesus.

Questions for Your Kids:

1. There were a couple miracles that happened in this story. Do you remember what they were? (*The first one is when the demon was cast out of the slave girl. The second one was when the earthquake came, breaking the bonds of the prisoners and opening the prison doors.*)

2. What was your favorite part of the story? What did you like about it? (*Have your children pick out their favorite parts. Was it something someone said? Was it when the spirit was cast out? When the earthquake happened? When the Philippian jailer became a Christian?*)

3. Years later, Paul wrote a letter to the church in Philippi. It is the letter of Philippians in our Bibles. Why do you think Paul would want to encourage them with a letter? (*The church needed encouragement because they were still being persecuted by others. They also needed more instruction about Jesus and Christianity because Paul was no longer there to teach them. We can still learn from this letter today.*)

> **Prayer:** Pray that God will help your family to memorize some of the verses in Paul's letter to the Philippians. Pray that just as God used this letter to encourage them long ago, he can use it to encourage your family to stay faithful to Jesus.

THE HEART OF HUMILITY
Teaching your children to put others first.

LESSON 2:
Meet Paul

Opening Thoughts:

- Do you remember what we learned about the Christians in Philippi in our last lesson? (*Have your kids see if they can remember anything about the slave girl, the jailer, Paul, Silas, the earthquake, or any other detail.*)

- Do you remember the name of the man who preached in Philippi and got thrown in prison? (*The apostle Paul*)

In this lesson we're going to learn more about Paul. He didn't go to prison just once for teaching about Jesus. He went many times. In fact, when he wrote a letter to his friends in Philippi, he was actually writing while he was in prison.

Scripture Reading: **Read Philippians 1:12-26**

Explanation: Paul was a man who learned how to be joyful, even when his situation was really bad. He was in jail for preaching about Jesus, but he still had joy. He was joyful knowing that because he was in prison, the Roman guards were hearing about Jesus. He was joyful knowing that he had set a good example for other Christians so they could tell others the good news of salvation. He was joyful even thinking about the possibility of death, because he knew when he died he would be with Christ forever.

Paul knew his time on earth was short. Some day he would die and be with Christ forever, but he knew God would not let him die until the time was right. Paul still had more work to do for Jesus, teaching and preaching at other churches.

Paul's greatest desire was to honor Jesus no matter what. If that meant being brave and dying for his faith, he would honor Jesus that way. If that meant living a little longer so he could strengthen and teach his fellow Christians, he would honor Jesus that way.

Questions for Your Kids:

1. Why do you think it would be hard to be in prison? (*Have your kids brainstorm what would make prison bad. They would be away from home and family. The food would be bad. They would not have their own bed. They couldn't see their friends. Maybe they would be treated poorly by the guards.*)

2. What made Paul joyful, even in prison? (*He thought about departing to be with Christ in heaven. He knew he was inspiring others to preach boldly about Christ. More people, like the Roman guards, were getting a chance to hear about Jesus because he was in prison.*)

3. What is one way God used Paul's time in prison to benefit even us today? (*It gave Paul time to write the letter to the Philippians, which is now in our Bible. God inspired Paul to write this letter so we could know more about what it means to follow Christ.*)

> Prayer: *Pray God will help your family to be joyful, even when things don't go your way. Ask God to help each person in your family to focus more on eternal and joyful things and less on temporary circumstances.*

THE HEART OF HUMILITY
Teaching your children to put others first.

LESSON 3:
The Problem in Philippi: Disunity

Opening Thought:

- What if I said to you, "Guess what! Tomorrow you get to do extra chores around the house!" What would you think?

- It seems weird for me to say "you *get to*," doesn't it? Usually we say "get" when we are about to do something fun, like, "I *get* to go to a movie," or "I *get* to eat ice cream." If you need to do chores, you'd probably say, "I *have* to do chores," not, "I *get to*."

But in today's passage Paul says something strange like that. Listen for it when I read it out loud.

Scripture Reading: **Read Philippians 1:27-30**

Explanation: Did you catch what Paul wrote at the end? Paul said they *get* to suffer for Christ. Paul didn't just say they were *called* to suffer for Jesus. He didn't say they *should* suffer for Christ. Paul said that suffering for Jesus was a gift. They *got* to suffer for him. Paul considered it an honor to be persecuted for believing in the One who died for him. That's how much he loved Jesus.

Paul says this is how we live lives worthy of the gospel. He's doesn't say we *are* worthy of the gospel: that is impossible. We are all unworthy because we are all sinful. But after we believe the gospel message about who Christ is and what He did for us, we should work hard to tell others about this, even if it means we are unpopular.

The world doesn't naturally like the gospel message about Jesus because it teaches them they need to repent of their sin, that they are guilty, and that God is their true Lord. The world killed Jesus because they didn't like His message. Paul spread that message and was always being persecuted. In this letter the Philippians are told to stand firm and spread the same message.

The problem is, they weren't standing *together* very well. There was grumbling and complaining going on among the Christians there. They were supposed to stand together like one army, setting their minds on the mission God had given them. Instead, they weren't united, and this made it hard to be bold.

Questions for Your Kids:

1. Do you remember the kind of suffering that Jesus went through when He was here on earth? What happened to him? (*Christ was told He was a liar and a blasphemer. He was rejected by His own people. He eventually died a horrible death on the cross.*)

2. Imagine you were in an army, but instead of everyone working together, all the soldiers were going different directions because they didn't like standing next to each other. Do you think you would be a very good army? (*No. If you are going to be able to fight the enemy, you need to work together. That was part of the problem in Philippi. They weren't standing together.*)

3. Have you complained or grumbled about someone recently? (*Parents, help your kids to think about the last time they did this. Remind them that God has called us to stand together and support each other, not divide.*)

> Prayer: Ask God to help you live lives worthy of the gospel, sharing Jesus with others, even when it isn't popular. Pray God will show you, as a family, ways you could be more united and stand together.

HEART OF HUMILITY
your children to put others first.

LESSON 4: The Solution: Humility

Opening Thought:

Last time we spoke about the problem in Philippi. They were supposed to stand together, helping each other to be bold and tell others about Jesus. Instead what was happening? (*They were not united. They were grumbling and complaining about each other.*)

The good news is, instead of just telling you to stop complaining and be united, the Bible actually tells us *how* to do that. That's what we're going to read about today.

Scripture Reading: Read Philippians 2:1-4

Explanation: Paul writes here that we are supposed to be humble or lowly. This means I should treat others around me as more significant than me. It means I should think about other people's problems and interests more than I think about my own.

In Paul's day, humility was not popular. People thought you were weak if you were humble. But God thinks differently than this. To God, humility means we remember that we are His creatures. When I remember I'm just a creature, I don't treat my interests like they are the most important things in the world. God is the center of the universe, and we are just one person in His big world. There are many other people with cares and concerns and problems. We are here to serve God and others, not ourselves.

Paul says humility is about really focusing on how we can be servants to other people, how we can help them, encourage them, and support them. Each time we walk into a room we should be saying in our heart, "God, show me how I can serve the people in here." Each time we wake up, we should be praying, "God, show me how I can serve people today in love."

Learning humility starts right here in our home. We see each other every day, so God gives us opportunities to serve each other every day. Imagine how great it would be if we all served each other in this home without any complaint!

Questions for Your Kids:

1. Who are the people you see every day or almost every day? (*Have your kids name off all the family and friends they see each day.*)

2. What are some ways you can be a servant to them? (*Then pick one or two of those people and ask your kids to think of ways they can serve those people in practical ways.*)

3. Why is it hard to remember to be humble and serve others? (*Because we are selfish. We like using our time for our own fun or interests. Often we don't "feel" like serving others.*)

4. If someone came to our home and saw us not being selfish but serving each other, how do you think they would react? (*Have you kids imagine what it would be like. The visitor might be amazed at the humility and wonder why we act so different than the rest of the world.*)

> Prayer: Pray that God would show your whole family how to be truly humble. Ask God to make your family an example of what it means to serve others.

THE HEART OF HUMILITY
Teaching your children to put others first.

LESSON 5:
Obstacles to Humility: Selfishness

Opening Thought:

Last time we talked about Paul's letter to the Philippians, we talked about a very important word: Humility.

What is humility? *(Humility is thinking less about your desires and more about the interests of others. It's about remembering that we're God's creatures. We are not the center of the world; God is. We are here to serve God and others, not ourselves.)*

But why is it so hard to be humble? That's what today's passage will tell us.

Scripture Reading: **Read Philippians 2:1-4**

Explanation: Paul writes there are two things in our hearts that fight against humility.

The first thing is selfish ambition. This means I have a sinful desire to focus on myself so much that I'm willing to ignore what others need or want, just so I can get my way.

The second thing is a desire for glory. I want others to serve me. I want others to pay attention to my needs. I want to be the most important person.

We all have these sinful attitudes in us. This is the reason why being humble is so hard to do sometimes: because humility is the opposite of selfishness. Because we are sinners, we all have a "me first" attitude.

And this is what the church in Philippi was dealing with. The reason there was fighting in the church is because each person was struggling with selfishness. They weren't willing to give up their own comforts or preferences or desires to serve others in the church.

Questions for Your Kids:

1. What are ways that we can be selfish around here? When are we the most selfish? *(Be honest with your kids about times you are the most selfish. When you are tired? Hungry? Busy? Ask them when they feel like they are the most selfish?)*

2. When was the last time you got into a fight with someone? Why did the argument get started? *(Help your kids remember a time recently when they were in an argument? Help them see how they were partially to blame because of their selfishness.)*

Prayer: Ask God to teach your family how to be humble. Pray that God will help your family to repent when you catch yourselves being selfish.

THE HEART OF HUMILITY
Teaching your children to put others first.

LESSON 6:
The Fruit of Selfishness: Grumbling & Disputing

Opening Thought:

In Philippians we've been learning about humility. Can you tell me what humility is? (*Humility is thinking less about your desires and more about the interests of others. It's about remembering that we are God's creatures. We are not the center of the world; God is. We are here to serve God and others, not ourselves.*)

Paul wrote this letter to help the Philippians not be selfish because selfishness is the opposite of humility. Today as we read more, we'll see what selfishness can lead to.

Scripture Reading: Read Philippians 2:14-16 and Exodus 16:1-3

Explanation: Grumbling, disputing, and complaining: this is what the children of Israel did only a few weeks after they left their slavery in Egypt. They sinfully complained against the leaders God had appointed. This means they were not united as a nation. Instead of being humble and respecting one another, they selfishly complained about one another.

Think about what a bad testimony this was to the nations around them. God had just done many great miracles that amazed everybody, rescuing his people from Egypt. But then his people were complaining that God wouldn't take care of them in the wilderness. The nations looking at Israel were probably thinking, "Can God take care of these people? Even Israel doesn't believe God will take care of them."

We can also be guilty of grumbling and complaining.

Let's say you invite a friend over to play. Let's also say that you really want to play with a favorite toy, but your friend really wants to play with that toy, too. As your friend grabs the toy, you might want it so bad that you grab it away from your friend, saying, "You can't play with that. This is *my* favorite toy." This makes your friend very upset so, you begin to get into an argument.

Paul writes that this is one way that selfishness can come out of us, when we want to have our own way so much, we begin arguing with others.

Or maybe you let your friend play with your favorite toy to be nice, but secretly you still really want it for yourself. So as you watch your friend play with your toy, you start to get a little upset as you think about all the fun you could be having with the toy. Eventually you start to get in a bad mood and soon you and your friend aren't having any fun at all.

Paul says this is another way selfishness can come out of us, when we want to have our way so much, we start to grumble against others.

Whether we argue or grumble, selfishness is the reason we do these things. Remember, selfishness is that me-first attitude that cares more about my own desires so much that I ignore the desires of others.

Instead, others in the world should look at us and think, "This person is full of joy. Even when things aren't going the way they want, they trust that God cares for them."

Questions for Your Kids:

1. Can you remember the last time you got into a bad mood? Do you remember what you were thinking about when that bad mood happened? (*Help your children think about the last time they grumbled about something. Help them to see what selfish motivations were driving that mood.*)

2. Do you know it is easy for me to get into a bad mood too? (*Talk about your own weaknesses in this area. Share a time when your own selfishness led you to grumble and complain. Share with your children about God's grace as well. Say, "The good news is there's hope for people like you and me. We all struggle with selfishness, but God can forgive us and give us power to live a different way."*)

> **Prayer:** Pray that God will help to reveal selfishness in your hearts. Ask God to forgive you and your children of your sins and give you power to live with humility.

THE HEART OF HUMILITY
Teaching your children to put others first.

LESSON 7: The Fruit of Humility: Oneness

Opening Thought:

As we've been reading Paul's letter to the Philippians, we've talked about a sinful tendency in all of us called selfishness. We can easily have a "me-first" attitude that leads to grumbling and arguing.

But we've also talked about humility. What is humility? (*Humility is the opposite of selfishness. It is thinking less about your desires and more about the interests of others. It's about remembering that we're God's creatures. We are not the center of the world; God is. We are here to serve God and others, not ourselves.*)

Today we'll read about why humility is so important.

Scripture Reading: **Read Philippians 2:1-4**

Explanation: Imagine what life would be like if no one was selfish, if everyone always was thinking about being a servant to everyone they met. It would mean that everywhere you go, people would be thinking about how they could help *you*. You would have a lot of servants! But you would also be focusing on everyone else around you, helping them to do the things they wanted to do. Everyone would be getting what they need.

Paul says this is what the church should be like. We should all be humble, not focusing on our differences or our disagreements, but focusing on loving Christ and loving others. When we are all humble together, we are *united*.

Paul says we are united when we set our minds on the same things, when we have the same love and passion, when we all live for the same purposes. When we all want to think and do things God's way, we are not only united, but we're moving in the opposite direction of selfishness.

This is a good description of what people will be like in heaven: when God takes all sin away from us, we will be totally focused on God and others. No more selfishness!

Until then, we are supposed to try to make our home and our church like a little colony of heaven. We want experience a little taste of heaven before we get there.

Questions for Your Kids:

1. Think about the last time you got angry at someone. Were you getting mad about things that also make God angry, or were you just mad because something wasn't going your way? (*Let your kids think about the last time they got mad. Let them tell the story. Help them to think critically about why they were so mad: was it because they were being somewhat selfish?*)

2. Think about the last time you played with someone and had a really good time: no one got upset about anything. When was that? (*Help your kids remember a time they played really well with siblings or friends. What made that time different? It was because they all agreed about what and how to play. The same is true for unity in the church or in your home: when everyone is thinking about the things God wants us to do, then we can all work together.*)

> **Prayer:** Pray that God will teach your family what it means be truly humble. Ask God to make your home into a place where you can get a taste of heaven.

THE HEART OF HUMILITY
Teaching your children to put others first.

LESSON 8:
Review: The Importance of Humility

Opening Thought:

Wouldn't it be wonderful if the whole world knew that Jesus was the Son of God? (*Have your kids imagine and describe what that would be like.*)

Everything we've been talking about humility is related to this. Today we're going to read from two passages. The first is Paul's letter to the Philippians, like we've been reading. The second is from a prayer Jesus prayed the night before He died.

Scripture Reading: Read Philippians 2:1-4 and John 17:20-23.

Explanation: In this prayer Jesus is praying for all the people who would later hear about Him through the teaching of His disciples. That's us. Today we read the words Jesus' disciples wrote about Him in the Bible, so this prayer is for us.

Jesus prayed that we would all be one, just as He is one with His Father in heaven. Jesus sent His Holy Spirit to us after He went to heaven, so now His Spirit comes to live inside every true Christian. We all have the same Spirit in us if we believe in Jesus. This is what makes us united to each other. God has made all Christians into brothers and sisters in Christ.

Jesus said if the world sees us united, they will believe that the Father sent Jesus and that God loves us. This is why we it is so important that we live like we are united: we want to show the world that Jesus is real. This is why it is so important that we learn to be humble: we don't want our selfishness to make the world say about us, "Oh, those Christians are no different than anyone else."

Christians are suppose to be different. This is why Paul wrote his letter to the Philippians. He wanted them to the fight any selfishness in their hearts that would cause division or arguments or complaining or grumbling.

Questions for Your Kids:

1. Can you remember what we've been talking about humility? What is humility? (*Humility is thinking less about your desires and more about the interests of others. It's about remembering that we're God's creatures. We are not the center of the world; God is. We are here to serve God and others, not ourselves.*)

2. If everyone in our home tried to be truly humble, how would that help us be more united? (*Have you kids picture what it would be like if they were never selfish, if they served others, and if everyone else in the home served them.*)

> **Prayer:** Pray that God will help you to learn humility through this passage in Philippians. Ask God to make your family a witness to the world that Jesus is real by the way you unselfishly treat each other.

THE HEART OF HUMILITY
Teaching your children to put others first.

LESSON 9:
Motivation for Humility: Encouragement in Christ

Opening Thought:

- Who are the people you are around the most? (*Have your child name the people they see nearly every day.*)

- Can you think of a person who is always with you, who never leaves you? (*Christ*)

Let's see what Paul writes to the Philippians about this.

Scripture Reading: **Read Philippians 2:1-4**

Explanation: It's one thing to say we need to be humble and serve others. It's another thing to show us *how* to do it. It is hard to put others first. The reason we are selfish is because our hearts are sinful. How does God actually change our hearts and make us *want* to be humble?

Paul tells us. He starts by saying that we have consolation or comfort from being "in Christ." Do you know what it means to be "in Christ"? It means we are united to Christ. It means Christ's Holy Spirit lives inside us. It means we belong to Christ. It means when God looks at us, He loves us like He loves Christ, His only Son.

Christ made a promise to His disciples before He went to heaven: I will never leave you nor forsake you. Paul says that knowing this should comfort us.

This should help us to be humble and have a servant heart. Think about when you are being selfish, those times when you are so focused on what you want that you forget about what other people want. What if, instead, you were thinking about the comfort you feel knowing that Jesus is always with you, knowing that you belong to Him. You would be thinking, "Christ is with me and loves me. I have no reason to be selfish. I can serve others and know that Christ is taking care of me."

Questions for Your Kids:

1. Why is it easy to forget that Jesus is with us all the time? (*Because we can't see Him. The Bible says Christians are supposed to walk by faith, not by sight [2 Corinthians 5:7]. This is something we need to practice. We should remind ourselves throughout the day that we are in Christ and that He is always with us.*)

2. What are some ways you can remind yourself that Jesus is with you all the time? (*There are many things you could do. Have a time of prayer every day to remind you. Sing songs throughout the day about Jesus. Recite Bible passages you've memorized throughout the day.*)

> Prayer: Ask God to remind you and your whole family that Jesus is with you all day long. Pray that you and your kids will feel the comfort of knowing that Christ is with you so your hearts are free to love and serve other people.

THE HEART OF HUMILITY
Teaching your children to put others first.

LESSON 10: Motivation for Humility: Comfort from Love

Opening Thought:

When someone says that they love you, what are ways you know that they really mean it? (*Have your kids talk about ways they know others really love them. How do others really show their love by their actions?*)

Love has a lot to do with what we've been learning about humility. Paul explains how in this passage.

Scripture Reading: **Read Philippians 2:1-4**

Explanation: Here Paul tells them, "If you really want to be humble, if you really want to be a servant to others, then think about God's love." He says they have comfort from love, so this should move them to be humble toward others.

How do we know that God loves us? Did He just *tell* us that He loves us? He certainly did that because He's spoken through prophets and through the Bible telling us that He loves us. But He has done *more* than just tell us. He shows us.

Paul wrote in another letter that the Father showed His love to us, in that while we were still sinners, Christ died for us (Romans 5:8). Can you imagine what that was like for the Father? He and His Son lived together forever. Before the world began, they have always been with each other and have always loved each other. There is no stronger love in the universe than the love they have for each other. But they also had a plan about how they were going to save us from our sins. The Father chose to send us His only Son. His Son became a man and then died a terrible death on the cross. Instead of punishing us for our sins, He chose to punish His only Son in our place.

Paul writes that He did this while we were still sinners. That means we weren't asking to be saved. We were just going our own way, not caring that we were sinning, not caring that we were offending God. Still, the Father chose to send the One He loves to die for us. Paul says this news should comfort us greatly.

Think about the times you aren't humble, the time when you feel selfish, when you just want to have your own way, or when you mistreat or speak bad to others because you are being selfish. What if, instead, you were thinking about how much God loves you? What if you were thinking about how the Father has showed His love to you?

Questions for Your Kids:

1. How would this change your attitude? (*Have your kids think about this. When we are focused on how much the Father loves us, we are inspired to show the same kind of love to others. God's love inspires us to be just like Him. We think less about ourselves and we think more about how we can serve others.*)

2. How did God show His love to us? What big sacrifice did He make? (*He chose to save us, even when we didn't ask for Him to do it, by sending His Son to die for us.*)

3. Have you ever sat down for a whole minute and just thought about the Father sending His Son to die? Let's try that. (*Have your kids sit very still, close their eyes, and think about Jesus dying on the cross. Ask them to sit still for 60 seconds and not make any sounds, but to just think about Jesus dying for them. Have them tell you what images were in their head when they are finished and how it made them feel.*)

> **Prayer:** Pray that God will show your family the length, breadth, height, and depth of God's love for you. Ask God to make all of you willing to sacrifice your own desires for each other the way God sacrificed for you.

THE HEART OF HUMILITY
Teaching your children to put others first.

LESSON 11: Motivation for Humility: Participation in the Spirit

Opening Thought:

Think of someone who is one of your best friends. What are the things you like to do together? *(Have your kids think of the shared activities they love to do with their friends.)*

Just like you enjoy certain kinds of activities with your friends, God wants us to enjoy the things we have in common with other Christians. And there is one thing we all have in common. Let's read about it.

Scripture Reading: **Read Philippians 2:1-4**

Explanation: Paul writes here that the Philippians all had fellowship or participation in God's Spirit. The Holy Spirit lives inside all Christians.

Do you believe in Jesus? If you really believe in Jesus, it means the Holy Spirit is inside you giving you the power to believe in Christ. He's the one who convinces you that Jesus is real and that God loves you.

Do you ever feel sorry for sinning? When you sin, do you feel guilty? If you really feel sorry for sinning, it means the Holy Spirit is the one inside you convicting you about the sins you commit. He's the one who makes us want to be forgiven and makes us want to do better.

All Christians share the same Holy Spirit. He's the one who binds us all together. We all belong to the same family because of the Holy Spirit.

It is a lot easier to be united with someone when you can think about the things you have in common with them. Just like when you play with your friends, you get along better when you all like to play the same things. Similarly, when we don't feel like serving others and putting them first, we should try to remember that as Christians we are all in the same family. We all have experienced the power of the Holy Spirit inside us. God has united us in one family by putting His Spirit in all of us. This makes us want to experience that unity.

Questions for Your Kids:

1. What are some of the ways you know the Holy Spirit is inside you? (*The Holy Spirit inspires us to believe in Jesus and repent of our sins.*)

2. What are good ways to remind ourselves that we all have the same Spirit inside us? (*We can talk to each other about what we're learning about Jesus. We can ask each other about the sins we feel convicted about. We can pray together and for each other. These activities remind us that the same Spirit is inside us, changing our hearts.*)

> **Prayer:** Ask God to help your family to remember that the Holy Spirit lives in your home. Pray that God will help your family experience the fellowship of the Spirit, helping you focus on the things the Spirit is teaching you.

THE HEART OF HUMILITY
Teaching your children to put others first.

LESSON 12:
Motivation for Humility: Affection & Sympathy

Opening Thought:

Have you ever felt really sorry for someone? When was that? (*Have your kids think of a time when they felt compassion for someone who was hurting or sad.*)

Have you ever felt so happy to be with someone that you gave them a big hug? (*Have your kids think of a time when that happened and share about it.*)

Remember those feelings you felt. They will come into play as we read our passage today.

Scripture Reading: **Read Philippians 2:1-4**

Explanation: Have you ever heard the expression "broken heart"? Or have you ever heard the expression "gut feeling"? These are ways we talk about strong emotions. When we have a broken heart, our heart really isn't broken. When we have a gut feeling, our stomach really isn't feeling anything. But when we feel strong emotions, our bodies react. Sometimes we cry. Sometimes we laugh. Sometimes we feel sick.

Paul asks his readers to remember the times when they felt strong emotions about God, or about him, or about one another. He says if they've ever felt strong affection or sympathy (which they had), this should help them to be humble toward each other.

Often when we feel really selfish and we want to have our own way, it is easy to forget the times we felt affection or sympathy for each other. Often we can feel deep love for someone one minute and then an hour later they are getting on our nerves, and we just want them to go away. It is at those times we need to remind ourselves about the affection we've shared with them. This helps us to treat them with kindness and humility.

Questions for Your Kids:

1. Do you remember what we said humility is? (*Humility is thinking less about your desires and more about the interests of others. It's about remembering that we're God's creatures. We are not the center of the world; God is. We are here to serve God and others, not ourselves.*)

2. Is it easier to be humble when we feel love for someone, or is it easier when we they are getting on our nerves? (*It feels easier when we feel love for them.*)

3. How can we be humble and servant-hearted toward someone we don't even know? (*We should try to remember the affection and sympathy we've experienced from others. There have been times when strangers have been kind to us. This should inspire us to be kind to others as well.*)

> Prayer: Pray that God will help your family to remember the times of affection and sympathy in your home. Ask God to give you a deeper love for one another.

THE HEART OF HUMILITY
Teaching your children to put others first.

LESSON 13: Motivation for Humility: The Joy of Others

Opening Thought:

When I say the word "rejoice" what do you think about? Can you show me what rejoicing looks like? *(Have you kids get up and "act out" rejoicing. Maybe they run around or dance or act goofy. Once they've calmed down again, continue.)*

Joy is a lot like happiness in some ways. We get a smile on our face when we are joyful. Today we're going to mention the word "joy." Be listening for it.

Scripture Reading: **Read Philippians 2:1-4**

Explanation: Many times in this letter, Paul mentions the idea of joy. He is joyful when he prays for his Christians friends in Philippi (1:4). He is joyful when he hears that people are preaching about Jesus throughout the world (1:18). He is joyful knowing that some day he might die for his faith (2:17). Knowing the Philippians are still faithful to God makes him joyful (4:1). Several times he tells them he wants them to be joyful in their faith (2:25; 3:1; 4:4).

But here he says, "If you want to make my joy complete, if you want to make my joy overflow, then be *united.*" He doesn't scold them by saying, "You better be humble and love each other." Instead, he reminds them of their love for him. They want to make Paul even more joyful, so he tells them to be humble and serve each other.

This is another reason why it is such a blessing to learn to be humble, because it brings joy to those who have taught us about Christ. For example, I feel joy when I sit down to tell you Bible stories. I feel joy when I hear you recite Bible verses to me. I feel joy when I know you're learning about God. But what really makes my joy overflow is when I see you thinking more about the desires of others and serving them, when I see you choosing to not be selfish. It shows me that your faith is real, that Jesus is really changing your heart.

Questions for Your Kids:

1. Who are the people who have taught you about Jesus in your life? *(Have your kids name anyone who might have been a teacher to them: parents, grandparents, older siblings, other relatives, preachers, pastors, teachers at church, etc.).*

2. Picture yourself 10 years from now or even 20 years from now. Now picture yourself as an older person serving God in some way, teaching others about Jesus, praying every day, and trying to be humble just like Jesus was. Picture those people who taught you about Jesus when you were a child. How happy would they be seeing you obedient to God? (*Have kids imagine what their life will be like in 10 or 20 years. Have them imagine what they will be doing then. Then remind them that whatever they are doing, the most important thing they can do is to be obedient to God and bring Him glory.*)

> Prayer: Pray that God will make your family joyful the way Paul was joyful. Ask Him to help you to make one another joyful by the way you treat each other.

THE HEART OF HUMILITY
Teaching your children to put others first.

LESSON 14: Review: 5 Motivations for Humility

Opening Thought:

Do you think digging a big hole in the ground would be very fun on a really hot day? (*No. It would be very hard work.*)

But what if I told you that just five feet under the ground is a huge treasure. There's a large treasure chest full of gold coins. If you got to that treasure, you would be rich.

Keep that in mind as we read.

Scripture Reading: **Read Philippians 2:1-4**

Explanation: God doesn't just tell us to be humble. He gives us the reasons why we should be humble. It's like digging that big hole: if we know there's a treasure under the ground, we will dig the hole, even if it is hard work. Similarly, if we know the blessings of being humble, we will want to do it.

As we've been reading Paul's letter to the Philippians, we've read about five reasons why we should strive to be humble. The first three reasons to focus our attention on God.

When we think about God, we have to remember that God is not just one person, but three. The Father, the Son, and the Holy Spirit are all divine. They have all been around before the beginning of the world. They are all perfect. They are all God.

First Paul talks about God the Son, saying we are "in Christ." We are united to Christ, we belong to Him, and He will never leave us or forsake us. Then he talks about God the Father, reminding us about His love. The Father sent His only Son to us to die for us, showing us how much He loves us. Then he talks about God the Holy Spirit. The Spirit is inside us inspiring us to repent of our sin and believe in Jesus. The Spirit is the one who binds us all together into one Christian family.

Paul tells them, "Think about the comfort and excitement you feel knowing that the Father, the Son, and the Spirit love you this way." It is amazing that God has done these things for us.

The first three reasons we should be humble focus our attention on God. But the last two focus our attention on others. First, he tells us to remember the times of affection and mercy we've felt toward each other. We should remember the times we have felt compassion for each other and how wonderful it is. Second, he reminds about those who have been our teachers and how we make them joyful when we live in a way that honors God.

When we think about these five things, they make us want to be humble. They make us want to serve others. God doesn't just say to us, "Be humble! Love others!" He loves us first. We honor God by loving others they way He loves us. It all starts by thinking about God and saying, "This kind of love is amazing! I love the way God has shown his love to me. I want to love others the same way. This is the kind of person I want to be."

Questions for Your Kids:

1. Who are the three persons of God? (*The Father, the Son, and the Holy Spirit*)

2. When God had the plan to save us from our sins, how do you think each person of God was involved? (*This is a big question, but get your kids to think about each person of the Trinity from what they know about them. The Father plans our salvation and sends His Son to die for us. The Son came to earth as a man and effected our salvation by dying for us. The Spirit comes to indwell us and apply salvation to us. All three are involved.*)

3. How do you think Paul wanted his readers to feel thinking about these things? (*Paul says we should be comforted knowing we are one with Christ, we should be moved and persuaded by God's love, and we should experience fellowship together because of the Spirit inside each of us. If we start each day thinking about these things, it will totally shape our attitudes.*)

> **Prayer:** Pray that God will help each person in your home know Him more. Ask God to help each person understand how each person of God shows His love to us.

THE HEART OF HUMILITY
Teaching your children to put others first.

LESSON 15:
The Example of Humility: Jesus, the One We Worship

Opening Thought:

- What are your favorite songs we sing in church? (*Have your children name them, or even sing them if they are in the mood.*)

- Do you think they sang songs about Jesus back when the church first started thousands of years ago? Yes, they did. In fact, we're going to read one now.

Scripture Reading: **Read Philippians 2:5-11**

Explanation: In this passage Paul is actually reciting a poem or song about Jesus. We do not know who wrote the song. It might have been Paul himself. It might have been someone else. But either way, Paul places this song at the center of his whole letter. He wants the Philippians to pay close attention to this song.

The Philippians lived in the Roman Empire, and in the Roman Empire there was one person who was the supreme ruler: Caesar. Caesar not only ruled over the whole empire, but he demanded that people worship him as a god. He told his subjects that he was from the gods, and his followers actually built temples to honor him. They sang songs about Caesar. They would say the phrase, "Caesar is Lord," to tell other people they were loyal to the emperor.

But Caesar was not a god. Paul knew that because he grew up learning from the Old Testament that there was no god but the true God of Israel. He grew up reading passages like Isaiah 45 where God says over and over, "I am God, and there is no other. I am the Lord, and there is no other."

In this song Paul is writing, he quotes the same chapter of Isaiah, which is all about God, and says it is also true about Jesus. The song says that at the name of Jesus every knee should bow, in heaven and on earth and under the earth, and every tongue should confess that Jesus Christ is Lord, to the glory of God the Father. Paul is saying that Jesus is one we should worship. Jesus is God and the true Lord, not Caesar.

Questions for Your Kids:

1. Do you think that singing a song like this would have gotten the Philippians in trouble with those who worshipped Caesar? (*Yes, it might have made them very unpopular or even gotten them in trouble with the law. Some like Paul had been arrested already for worshipping Jesus.*)

2. Do you think that singing a song like this would get the Philippians in trouble with Jewish people who didn't believe in Jesus? (*Yes. The Jews who didn't believe in Jesus thought it was blasphemy to say Jesus was equal to God. When they saw Jesus they believed He was only a man.*)

3. How do we know that Jesus is God? (*God's Word says that Jesus is God; this passage is one example. Also, Jesus said that He is God, and He proved it by the miracles He did. Have your kids talk about some of the miracles of Jesus they remember.*)

> **Prayer:** Ask God to help your family to love Jesus more and more every day. Pray that God will help your family to understand who Jesus really is and what He has done for us.

THE HEART OF HUMILITY
Teaching your children to put others first.

LESSON 16: The Example of Humility: Jesus, the One Who Let Go

Opening Thought:

Picture the most powerful ruler in the world. Picture him sitting on a high throne and everyone in the world coming to him to serve him. Picture him wearing a golden crown with the most expensive jewels in it. No one is more powerful than him. Now picture him taking off his crown, putting on normal clothes, and walking around the street like just anyone else. People might not even recognize him.

Today we're going to see how this applies to Jesus.

Scripture Reading: **Read Philippians 2:5-11**

Explanation: If I were to point at a chair and say, "That is in the form of a chair," what do I mean? I mean it has all the things a chair is supposed to have. It has legs. It has a back. It has a seat. It is shaped a certain way. It is a chair in every way.

That's what Paul means when he says Jesus is in the "form of God": He has all the essential qualities of being God. God knows everything; so does Jesus. God is all-powerful; so is Jesus. God is everywhere and sees everything; so does Jesus. God is perfectly wise; so is Jesus. God has always existed; so has Jesus. Jesus is 100% divine. He is equal to God in every way because He *is* God. Before Jesus was born as a man, He existed as God.

But Paul says Jesus didn't cling to His rights as God. He could have stayed in the same position of glory forever. But He didn't. He chose to do something amazing. He let go of his majesty, rights, and privileges as God and become a man.

He is like the king who stepped down from his throne, took off his crown, put on street clothes, and walked around like a normal man. Just because he looked different doesn't mean he wasn't still the king. He was still the same man. But that king was setting aside his privileges as king. He wouldn't be surrounded by the same comforts. People wouldn't give him the same respect. People would just treat him like they treat everyone else.

This is one way Jesus was so humble. He didn't cling to his rights. He didn't say to Himself, "I'm God! There's *no* way I'm going to become a man." He didn't say, "I like it here in heaven. There's no way I'm leaving." He didn't cling to his privileges as God. He let go.

This is what it means for us to be humble and serve others. We surrender our rights. We don't say, "But I want others to pay attention to *me*. There are things I want to do. There's *no way* I'm going to act like someone else's servant." Being humble means letting go of the things we want to do and gladly serving others.

Questions for Your Kids:

1. When we say Jesus was in the form of God, what does that mean? (*It means Jesus is like God in every way. Have you kids talk about some of the attributes of God, like omniscience, omnipotence, omnipresence, etc.*)

2. What would have happened if Jesus decided to cling to his rights as God? (*He would never have come to earth as a man. This means He would have never died on the cross for our sins, and we would not be forgiven for all our sins.*)

3. If someone needs help, but we're more focused on our own desires and rights at the time, are we *more* or *less* likely to help them? (*Less likely. If we cling to our rights, we want others to pay attention to us and serve us. But if we surrender our desires, we are free to serve others around us.*)

> Prayer: Pray God will make you and everyone in your home more like Jesus, willing to give up our desires and comforts to serve one another. Ask God to change your hearts so you don't desire to cling to your rights, but so you are willing to give them up to serve others.

THE HEART OF HUMILITY
Teaching your children to put others first.

LESSON 17:
The Example of Humility: Jesus, the True Man

Opening Thought:

- Jesus is God, right? (*Yes. Have your kids talk about what they remember from the last lesson.*)

- So, when Jesus was on earth, if He was God, do you think He got hungry? (*Yes.*) Thirsty? (*Yes.*) Tired? (*Yes.*)

He experienced all those things and more. Let's read more of our text about that.

Scripture Reading: **Read Philippians 2:5-11**

Explanation: Last time we talked about how Jesus was in the form of God, but He didn't cling to his rights and privileges as God. Instead He let go.

Paul says here that when He let go of those rights He emptied Himself and became a man. Notice Paul doesn't say that He emptied Himself *of* anything in particular. He didn't stop being God. Rather Paul means Jesus poured Himself out, giving *all* of Himself to us. He didn't hold back anything.

And He did it in a most unique way: He became a human being. For a little over 30 years, Jesus lived as a man among us. He didn't look like God to the people who saw Him. It's like when the sun goes behind a cloud. The sky gets darker and we don't see how bright the sun really is. But if we go up into the sky above that cloud, the sun is shining as bright as ever. That's what Jesus did: He hid the fullness of His glory from us. Jesus hid His divine glory for a short time and chose to live as a man.

This means He experienced life like we do. Paul says He was found in fashion as a man. This means He was a normal looking man. He had to be born the same way we all were born. When He came out of His mom's body, He was little and helpless, just like all babies are helpless. He got hungry and tired. When He got hurt, He felt pain. He grew like we all grow. He experienced all the emotions we do: pain, sadness, happiness, crying, laughter, loneliness. He was surrounded by the same sinful world we live in.

This is the kind of humility we should have. One of the best ways to serve others is not just to help them from a distance but to join them in their suffering. If we see someone needing help, instead of just handing them something they might need, we can also sit with them, talk with them, listen to them, cry with them, laugh with them, and be their friend. This is what Jesus did for us: He joined the human race and experienced what it is like to be a human being.

Questions for Your Kids:

1. Do you think Jesus had to learn things just like you have to learn things? (*Yes. Luke 2:52 says He grew in wisdom. He had to learn how to talk, walk, eat, read, and write.*)

2. Do you think that since Jesus was God He had to obey His parents, too? (*Yes. Luke 2:51 says He was submissive to His parents. Isn't it wild to think about? Jesus was the one who created Joseph and Mary, and yet He chose to be obedient to His heavenly Father and submit to His parents just like all children should.*)

3. Does Jesus know what it's like to be a child like you? (*Yes. When we pray to God we can remember that Jesus remembers what it's like to be a kid. He remember what it's like to grow up. When we're frustrated about something because we wish we were older or bigger, Jesus understands that. We can take comfort knowing that.*)

> **Prayer:** Pray to God for opportunities to serve people the same way Jesus did. Ask God to show you ways to serve others in your family and among your friends who need you to join them in their struggles.

THE HEART OF HUMILITY
Teaching your children to put others first.

LESSON 18: The Example of Humility: Jesus the Servant

Opening Thought:

The last night that Jesus was alive, He did a very special thing during a meal with His disciples. He got up from the table, wrapped a towel around his waist, and start washing the disciples' feet. This was a very dirty job because every one back then wore sandals and the roads were all dusty and dirty. What Jesus did was a job that only servants did. The disciples were shocked.

Today we're going to read about why Jesus did that.

Scripture Reading: **Read Philippians 2:5-11**

Explanation: Remember earlier we talked about how Jesus is in the very form of God. Jesus has all the qualities that make God who He is.

Paul uses the same expression again, only this time he says Jesus took the form of a *servant*. Jesus didn't just leave heaven and hide all of His glory. He didn't just become a man and experience all the pains of living on earth. He also became a servant among us. He left the highest position in the universe and chose the lowest position on earth.

The word "servant" in this passage refers to someone who was a bondslave. If you were a servant to someone back then, and you really liked working for them, you could go up to them and say, "I want to serve you for the rest of my life. I choose to be your servant until the day I die." That person would then be a bondslave as long as they lived.

Like a bondslave, Jesus didn't *have* to be our servant. He *chose* to be. He didn't have to serve other people. He is God. He could have come to earth as a king, wore fine clothes, ate the best food, and demand that other people serve Him. He deserved that kind of treatment because He is God. But He didn't. He *chose* to serve others.

Jesus lived like a servant. Bondslaves owned nothing of their own. They were poor. Jesus was born into a poor family, born in a dirty stable where animals lived, and lived in a small town. To our knowledge, He didn't own land, a house, or any riches. Even the day He died, He was buried in a borrowed tomb. If you had been there to see Jesus, you would have thought by looking at Him that He was an ordinary man. This is how humble Jesus was.

Questions for Your Kids:

1. What does it mean to be a bondslave? (*A bondslave was a voluntary servant who chose to be someone's servant for life.*)

2. We talked about Jesus washing the disciples' feet. Can you think of any other ways that He served people? (*Have your children try to remember any stories they know from the life of Jesus. He healed people of their sicknesses, He taught them, He fed them, and He would be with the people for long hours to make sure He served them all.*)

3. One of the reasons we often don't help people is because we are selfish. We are only thinking about the stuff we want to do. How does this story about Jesus help us to be different? (*Jesus gives us an example to follow. Because we are so touched by His love for us by being willing to serve us, we don't mind serving others.*)

> **Prayer:** Ask God to help your family appreciate more the surrender of Jesus' will to serve others. Pray that God will change your hearts to help you be less selfish and more focused on the needs of others.

THE HEART OF HUMILITY
Teaching your children to put others first.

LESSON 19: The Example of Humility: Jesus, Who Obeyed to the End

Opening Thought:

As we're learning this passage in the book of Philippians, what we're talking about today may be the most important thing we discuss. Don't miss this.

Can you remember a time when you felt a lot of pain in your body somewhere? (*Have your children think about the last time they were sick or the last time they got hurt. Have them describe the experience.*)

Do you know Jesus also experienced great pain? It is a pain you could never imagine.

Scripture Reading: **Read Philippians 2:5-11**

Explanation: Paul writes here that Jesus became obedient to death, even the death of the cross. You've probably seen a cross before. Sometimes there are crosses people put inside or on the top of their churches. Sometimes people wear little crosses around their necks as jewelry. But in Paul's day, no one would ever think of doing that.

Dying on a cross was one of the worst ways to die. It was considered impolite to talk about crucifixion because it was so horrible.

The day Jesus was crucified, they first beat Him with whips and rods that ripped into his skin. Then they made a crown full of thorns that they pressed into His head, stabbing through his scalp. He was beaten so badly, people could hardly recognize Him.

They then strapped Him down to the wood of a cross and nailed his wrists and feet to the wood. This was very painful. Then they lifted the cross up for everyone to see. It was a slow, painful death.

It was also humiliating. Most everyone they crucified was naked. Some people would come just to laugh at the victims and make fun of them. If you were crucified, the Jewish people considered you cursed by God. They reserved crucifixion for the worst of criminals.

Jesus was willing to do this because He was being obedient to the Father: this was what the Father wanted Him to do. In the next lesson we'll talk about why His Father wanted Him to do it, but for now, think about how Jesus was so willing to obey God even when it was really hard to do. In fact one of the last prayers Jesus prayed on the cross, right before He died, was this, "Father, into your hands I commend my spirit." He was devoted to His Father right up to the minute He died.

Questions for Your Kids:

1. What do you think the worst part of crucifixion would be? (*Have your kids imagine a little. Have them think about the physical pain and the humiliation of being crucified.*)

2. What would have been a more comfortable way to die? (*Most anything would have been easier. Jesus could have died of old age in His sleep, surrounded by friends and family in a comfortable bed. It would have been a more noble way to die. Jesus was perfect and deserved to be treated like a king, but He chose to be treated like a criminal.*)

3. Does God sometimes ask us to do things that are hard to do? Like what? (*Yes. In this passage, God is asking us to be humble like Christ. He wants us to set aside our own desires and serve other people. That can be hard to do because we are selfish.*)

> **Prayer:** Pray to God to make the story of the cross more real to your whole family. Ask God to humble your hearts as you think about how obedient Jesus was, and ask God to give you the same heart of obedience.

THE HEART OF HUMILITY
Teaching your children to put others first.

LESSON 20: The Example of Humility: Jesus, Who Died for Our Sins

Opening Thought:

Can you think of a time you felt really scared in the dark? (*Have your kids imagine a time when they felt scared at night or in a dark room.*)

The dark is scary to some people because you feel helpless in the dark. You can't see to move around. You don't know if something is in the dark you might trip over.

On the cross, Jesus experienced a darkness that scared everybody around Him. Let's read about it.

Scripture Reading: **Read Philippians 2:5-11 and Mark 15:33-41**

Explanation: Jesus' crucifixion is hard to think about because we know how bad crucifixion was. It was humiliating. It was painful. It was one of worst ways to die people have ever invented.

But one of the worst pains of Jesus' death was the loneliness. The night He was arrested, all His disciples ran away so they wouldn't be arrested as well. The crowds who used to celebrate how wonderful Jesus was, they weren't there to support Him. By the time He died, only a few disciples were close to the cross.

But the worst loneliness of all was when His Father turned away from Him. From about noon until 3:00 in the afternoon, a mysterious darkness covered the land. The sun was covered. Then Jesus cried out, "My God, My God, why have you forsaken me?"

When Jesus went to the cross, His Father's plan was to punish Jesus for the sins of others. Jesus was going to experienced the punishment we deserve for our sins. We all deserve to be cut off from God forever. We all deserve to go to hell for our sins. What Jesus experienced on the cross was like hell. The Father turned His own Son over to cruel Romans and He let them kill Him. The Father turned His face away and refused to help His Son. That day Jesus experienced what it is like to be cut off from the Father and His loving care.

Jesus was experiencing something on the cross He had never felt before. For all eternity He and the Father had been together. Even when He was born as a man, He listened to His Father, and every day they spoke together. His Father loved Him. But for a few hours on the cross, Jesus knew what it was like to be forsaken by God.

Jesus obeyed His Father's plan so that we would be forgiven for all our sins. All who come to Jesus now can be forgiven for everything they did wrong because Jesus has taken the punishment for sin in our place. Jesus can forgive and save anyone who comes to Him.

Questions for Your Kids:

1. Can you think of a time when you have felt really lonely? (*Have your kids think of a time when they felt lonely and have them share it with you.*)

2. What do you think it would be like to be shut out from God's presence forever? (*This may be difficult for your children to imagine, but help them to think about all ways God shows His mercy to us now, all the comforts He gives us. Imagine never having those comforts. Help them think about how amazing it would be to see God's face. Help them to think about not getting to see Him, but being cut off from God forever.*)

3. How do you feel about Jesus' choice to die on the cross for other people's sins? (*Perhaps your children will express gratefulness, sadness, feel convicted about their sin, or feel humbled. Give them time to express how they feel. If the time feels right, ask them if they want to pray to God right now to ask Him to forgive them of their sins.*)

> **Prayer:** Thank God for sending His Son to die for the sins of the world. Ask Jesus to help your family to think deeply about the cross and what Jesus went through.

THE HEART OF HUMILITY
Teaching your children to put others first.

LESSON 21: The Example of Humility: Jesus, the Exalted One

Opening Thought:

After Jesus died on the cross, how do you think the disciples felt? *(Have your children talk about how scared or lonely the disciples were, or how many questions they might have had.)*

Today we get to read about the great things that happened next.

Scripture Reading: Read Philippians 2:5-11 and Matthew 28:1-10

Explanation: The story of Jesus' life on earth doesn't end with His death on the cross. At the end of his song, Paul writes about the exciting events that happened afterward.

Paul writes that God highly exalted Jesus. He did this when He raised Jesus from the dead. On the day of the resurrection, women went to the tomb. As the sun was rising, an angel came down, causing a great earthquake, and moved the stone away from the entrance of the tomb so that anyone could see that the Jesus' body was gone. As the women went back, they actually saw Jesus alive again walking on the road. They were filled with joy. He told the women to tell the other disciples and that He would appear to all of them later.

That's exactly what He did. He appeared many times to the disciples of the next 40 days. He spoke with them, ate with them, and taught them. Then 40 days after His resurrection, standing on the Mount of Olives, Jesus was taken up into heaven right in front of them. God took Jesus back home to sit at His right hand forever.

Paul writes that the Father bestowed on Jesus a name above every name, and that name is "Lord." He crowned Jesus the master and ruler of the world. And some day every knee will bow before Jesus. Everyone will bow down in front of Jesus and recognize that He is the real Lord of the universe: every angel in heaven, every person who has ever lived, and even evil angels and evil people will call Him Lord.

The Father exalted His Son this way because He was so obedient to Him. He humbled Himself completely. He emptied Himself and became a servant to all, dying the most humiliating death on the cross.

This is why we can humble ourselves and serve others, because we know that God promises to exalt everyone who humbles themselves. We can never humble ourselves as much as Jesus did, but we can lay aside our own interests and serve others knowing that at the right time, God will exalt us (Matthew 23:12; 1 Peter 5:6).

Questions for Your Kids:

1. How do you think you would have reacted if you saw an angel coming down from heaven to roll away the stone? (*Have your kids act out how they would react. Would they have fainted like the guards? Would they scream? Would they hide their eyes?*)

2. Do you think it was hard for the disciples to believe that Jesus really was alive again after He died on the cross? (*Your kids might say yes, and this is true. Some doubted that Jesus really could be alive again. Your kids might say no, and this is true as well: eventually Jesus convinced them that He was alive by appearing to them many, many times.*)

3. Does God promise to exalt us if we humble ourselves and serve others? (*Yes. Jesus promised that the last will be first and the first will be last. The person who serves the most will be awarded the greatest in eternal world to come.*)

> **Prayer:** Ask God to give your family the same mindset of humility that Jesus had. Pray that God will help your family to always remember that God rewards those who serve Him, just like the Father rewarded His Son.

THE HEART OF HUMILITY
Teaching your children to put others first.

LESSON 22: Review: The Example of Christ

Opening Thought:

- What do you like to build stuff with? (*Ask your kids about their favorite building-block toy. It could be Lego® brand toys or Mega Bloks®. It could be Magna Tiles®, Lincoln Logs®, or even just using household furniture and blankets to make a fort.*)

- If I told you you had to build the biggest structure possible, do you know how you would build it strong so it wouldn't fall down? (*Get them to describe what they would build and help them realize that they would need help building something really big.*)

Things are easier to do if we have someone we can follow. If someone was right next to you, not just telling you what to do but showing you so you could copy them, it would be a lot easier. That's what this passage is all about: copying Jesus.

Scripture Reading: Read Philippians 2:5-11

Explanation: Remember, the whole point of this section Paul's letter to the Philippians is that they learn what it means to be truly humble. Humility is thinking less about your desires and more about the interests of others. It's about remembering that we're God's creatures, that we are not the center of the world; God is. We are here to serve God and others, not ourselves.

The ultimate example of humility is Jesus. This is why Paul writes out this song or poem about Jesus, to remind them about how humble Jesus was.

Paul says they should have the same mind in them that was in Christ. They should think the same way Jesus thought. There were five things Jesus did as a humble man.

- First, He knew who is was. Jesus is 100% God. He has been God forever. He will be God forever. He was full of glory and majesty. This was where He started.
- Second, He chose to let go of His privileges. He didn't need to cling to His privileges and His majesty as God. He gave up his crown of glory.
- Third, He chose to be a servant. He didn't come into the world looking like a king to be served by others. He came to serve others. He chose to have the attitude of a servant to others around Him.
- Fourth, He gave all of Himself. Paul says He emptied Himself, He poured Himself out and became a man. He chose to join us on earth and share all the hard experiences we have as people. He finally gave all of Himself on the cross, experiencing the most humiliating death possible.

- Fifth, He looked forward to the reward. The Father exalted Jesus above everyone else because He obeyed. Jesus knew that His Father exalts the humble, so He looked forward to the day He would be exalted again.

These are the same five things we get to do.

- First, remember who you are. Just like all people, you are made in the image of God. If you choose to serve other people and be humble, you don't need to worry about what anyone else thinks about you, because God says about you, "I made you. You are made in my image. You are my special creation."
- Second, choose to let go of your privileges. You could spend all your time thinking about yourself, but instead God wants us to know that He will take care of us. We can think less about our desires and more about what others need because God knows what we need.
- Third, choose to be a servant. Don't wait for others to serve you. Whenever you are with others, think about ways you can serve them instead.
- Fourth, give everything you've got. We can never give as much as Jesus gave, but when we think about Jesus becoming a man and dying on the cross, it should inspire us to say, "I want to be a person like that. I want to give everything I can to serve others. Jesus is the kind of person I want to be."
- And fifth, look to reward. As we serve others, we can remember that God exalts the humble. Some day, He will crown us with glory and honor.

Questions for Your Kids:

1. What are the ways Jesus served other people? (*Have your kids think of stories from the Gospels they know about Jesus healing people, feeding people, teaching them, etc.*)

2. Why is it hard to give up the things we want to do to serve others? (*It is difficult because we are selfish. We want other people to serve us instead.*)

3. Do you ever think about the day that Jesus will come back to reward his followers? (*Have your kids talk about what they imagine that day will be like.*)

> **Prayer:** Ask God to teach your family to have the mind of Christ. Pray that He will help you to recognize when you need to set aside your desires to serve other people.

THE HEART OF HUMILITY
Teaching your children to put others first.

LESSON 23: Motivation for Humility: We are Saved from Sin

Opening Thought:

If a teacher tells the class that she wants everyone to work on an assignment quietly at their desks and then she leaves the room for 15 minutes, what do you think would happen? (*The students will probably start goofing off and talking to each other. When the teacher gets back, many of the students might not even be done with their assignments.*)

Sometimes we obey better when our parents or our teachers are around. When we think nobody is watching us, it is easy to forget what we're supposed to do. It is easy to start doing our own thing.

Paul mentions this in our passage today.

Scripture Reading: **Read Philippians 2:12-13**

Explanation: Paul says the Philippians were extraordinary Christians, because they didn't just obey God when Paul was around. They continued to obey God even after Paul left. They weren't obeying God just for show. They weren't obeying God just to make Paul happy. They were obeying God because they *wanted* to obey Him.

Paul says, "You've proven to me that you really want to obey God. That means God has really changed your hearts. He has rescued you from the power of sin in your heart. So now work out your own salvation." That's an interesting idea: work out your own salvation. What does that mean?

When the Philippians had heard the gospel, they believed in Jesus, and God broke the power of sin in their hearts. They used to think only about themselves and be selfish. But now they *wanted* to obey God and serve others because God had changed their desires. So Paul says, live out your salvation. God has given you the desire and power to be humble like Christ, so now live it out!

It's like if you had a gold mine in your backyard. Deep down in the mine is tons of gold. You just have to go out there and start digging. It's the same way with our salvation from sin. We are already saved from sin if we believe in Christ. We already have the Spirit of God inside us. We just need to bring out what God has already put inside us. That's how we have the power to be humble like Christ.

Questions for Your Kids:

1. What does it mean to be saved from sin? (*It means many things. First, it means we are forgiven for our sins. Second, it means we have been set free from the power of sin. It also means that one day we will totally be free from the presence of sin when God transforms the whole world.*)

2. Who are the people you spend the most time with? (*Have your kids talk about the people they see the most: friends, family, or neighbors.*)

3. Think of one of those people. What are ways you can encourage each other to be humble like Christ? (*Have your children think of one of the people they mentioned—a sibling, a friend from church, you, anyone—and then think of ways they could serve one another. By being an example of humility to each other, we help one another to remember the importance of being like Christ.*)

Prayer: Ask God to give your family the confidence of knowing that Christ has set you free from the power of sin. Pray He helps you to choose to be humble because you now have the power to be humble like Christ.

THE HEART OF HUMILITY
Teaching your children to put others first.

LESSON 24: Motivation for Humility: God is at Work Among Us

Opening Thought:

Picture a little kid walking with his mom at the grocery store with a shopping cart. The little kid gets up behind the cart and is barely tall enough to reach the bar. He pushes the cart along, really happy that he can be a big boy and push the cart all by himself. What he doesn't realize is that his mom is also holding on to the cart and guiding it along, making sure it doesn't bump into anything, and pushing it forward. The child just feels like he's the one doing the work, but its actually his mom pushing the whole time.

That's how it is with us and God. We are commanded to obey God and be like Christ, but it is actually God inside us, changing us, and making us able to do it. That's what we'll read about in today's passage.

Scripture Reading: Read Philippians 2:12-13

Explanation: Paul writes here, it is God at work in us. He is doing two things in us. First, He is moving our wills. That means He is changing our desires so that we *want* to do the things He wants. Second, He is helping us to work. That means He is giving us the *power* to do what He wants.

God both commands us to change and causes us to change. God isn't finished with us. He isn't done changing us. He is at work even right now, changing our desires and giving us the power to obey Him.

Because of this, Paul says we should be filled with fear and trembling. Think about the One who is in you, changing you. It is *God* doing it. This is the same God who created the world. This is the same God who is totally perfect. This is the same God who divided the Red Sea. This is the same God who has the power of life and death. This is the same God who raised Jesus from the dead. And it is the same God who will send Jesus again to judge the whole world. This is the God who is at work in us and among us to change us. This should amaze us if we really think about it.

We should also be excited about this. It might seem hard to be humble and serve others like Jesus, but when we remember that the all-powerful God is inside us, shaping us into the people He wants us to be, we should be confident. We should say to ourselves, "If God wants me to serve others, I know I will have the power to do it. I'm going to serve others like Christ did, knowing that God is the one helping me."

Questions for Your Kids:

1. How powerful is God? (*God is all-powerful. Nothing is too difficult for Him.*)

2. What does it mean that God is at work in us to will and to work? (*It means God is changing our desires so we want to obey Him and giving us the power to obey Him.*)

3. Does it sometimes seem like its really hard to be humble and want to serve others? (*If you children say no, remind them of the last time you saw them bickering or complaining about something. This is a form of selfishness. If they say yes, remind them that God is at work in them to change their hearts, so this should encourage them.*)

> **Prayer:** Ask God to remind your family every day that He is at work in you and among you to change your hearts and minds. Pray for God to make you into humble servants just like Christ.

THE HEART OF HUMILITY
Teaching your children to put others first.

LESSON 25:
Motivation for Humility: Pleasing God

Opening Thought:

Let's say there was a kid who ran away from home because he didn't want to have to obey his mom and dad anymore. So one night he snuck out of the house and started living on the street, trying to live all by himself. His mom and dad would be worried sick, hoping some day to find their son.

One day the boy gets tired of living on the street and feels really bad for leaving home, so he walks back home. He's tired of being cold and hungry. Most of all, he misses his mom and dad. When his parents see him, they are overjoyed. They give him a huge hug and kiss and bring him inside where he is warm and safe again.

Think about that story today when we read our passage.

Scripture Reading: Read Philippians 2:12-13 and 2 Corinthians 5:6-10

Explanation: Paul says when we obey God and live more like Christ, we are doing it for God's good pleasure.

Think of the story I just told you about the boy who ran away. When he ran away, did he stop being their son? No. He was still their son when he ran away. He was still their son when he was sleeping on the street. He was still their son when he was cold and hungry. He was still their son when he walked home. And he was their son when he was safe at home again.

He never stopped being their son, and his parents always loved him. But were they always pleased with him? Were they pleased that he ran away? Were they pleased that he didn't want to live at home anymore? No. They were not pleased.

It's the same way with us and God. When we are forgiven of all our sins, we become God's children. We are His. God becomes our Father. But when we disobey God, He can still be displeased with us. This does not mean He stops being our Father, and it does not mean God stops loving us, but it does mean He wishes we would obey Him.

Similarly, when we obey God we please Him as our Father. This is another reason why we should be humble like Christ: because we know that God is pleased with us.

Questions for Your Kids:

1. Can you become my child "more" if you obey me more? (*No. Your child will always be your child, no matter how much he or she obeys you.*)

2. Can you ever stop being my child by disobeying me? (*No. Your child will always be yours, no matter how much he or she disobeys you.*)

3. Can you please me by the good things you do around here? (*Yes. Parents are very pleased with their children do what they are told.*)

4. Can we please our heavenly Father by the good works we do? (*Yes. We can bring God pleasure by the good things we do.*)

5. Do we please God when we serve others and try to be humble like Christ? (*Yes. This is exactly what Paul is telling us to do in this passage: to have the same mind that Christ had when He came to earth to be a servant.*)

6. There's a big difference between trying to please God to get Him to love you and trying to please God because you know He is already your Father. Do you see the difference? (*Help your children to understand the difference if they don't. Obeying God as a believer in Christ does not make God love you more or make you more a son or daughter of God. God is already our Father. But by obeying God, we still bring Him pleasure the same way obeying parents brings them pleasure.*)

Prayer: Ask God to teach you be happy knowing that every time we serve God, we are bringing pleasure to Him. Pray that God will help you remember that every time we humbly serve others, we are bringing a smile to His face.

THE HEART OF HUMILITY
Teaching your children to put others first.

LESSON 26: Motivation for Humility: Being Blameless Witnesses

Opening Thought:

Let's say you got a small candle and you took it outside on a sunny day. Then you held the candle up in the air so the sun was behind it. Next to the sun, the candle wouldn't look very bright at all. You wouldn't even be able to see the candle anymore because the sun would be so bright if you looked right at it.

But take the same candle outside on a dark, cloudy night and it will look very different. The candle would be bright enough to light up the space all around you. It would be the brightest thing you could see.

Today, in the passage we read, you'll learn how you are a lot like that candle.

Scripture Reading: **Read Philippians 2:14-18**

Explanation: Paul is writing to the Philippians about how their humility and servant-hearts make them shine like lights in the world. Compared to Jesus, the Philippians don't look very humble. Jesus was the humblest man that ever lived. They are like a candle next to the sun. Standing next to Jesus, they don't look very humble.

But remember what the surrounding world looked like. Paul said they were living in a place that was crooked and twisted. Everyone around them worshipped false gods. They did not like Christians, and they did not like the gospel of Christ. The sinful world around us is dark.

This is why even just a little humility can be like a candle on a dark night. Compared to the world around us, when we try to be like Christ this makes us stand out. Paul says when we try to be humble and servant-hearted like Christ, we shine like lights in the world. People look at us and say, "They are different. They aren't selfish like the rest of us. They don't grumble and complain. They are living a different way."

As we share with others about Jesus, our lives should reflect what we say. If we say Jesus is the Son of God who forgives us of our sins and changes our lives, we should live in a way that shows that Jesus is real to us. This is another reason why we should strive to be humble and serve others: it shows the surrounding world that Christ is real.

Questions for Your Kids:

1. When you see another kid grumble and complain all the time, what do you think about him or her? (*Have your children imagine what they think when they see someone else complain a lot. We tend to think, "I wish that person would stop being so negative," or "That person is really selfish."*)

2. If you met someone who never complained, who always served you, always said kind things to you, and never acted rude of selfish, would you want to be around that person more? (*Yes. We love to be around people who put others first.*)

3. Do you think more people would want to listen to us talk about Jesus if we were like that? (*Yes. Our lives should go with the message we speak. If we say Jesus can change our hearts, then we should live in a way that shows it.*)

> **Prayer:** Ask God to make your family shine like lights in your community. Pray that God will help your family to serve others more so you can be better witnesses to others about the kindness and humility of Christ.

THE HEART OF HUMILITY
Teaching your children to put others first.

LESSON 27:
Motivation for Humility: The Word of Life

Opening Thought:

Imagine a man climbing a mountain with a rope tied around his waste. The rope goes all the way to the top of the mountain and is firmly tied to a big rock. Imagine him gripping each rock as he climbed higher and higher, and then all of a sudden, one of the rocks breaks off. He loses his grip and begins falling down and suddenly the rope catches him. He is very happy to have that rope because without it, he might have been hurt or died.

Now imagine him reaching up and climbing that rope so he can find a safe place to grab on to the mountain again. Picture that in your mind, how tightly he's holding that rope as we read our passage today.

Scripture Reading: **Read Philippians 2:14-18**

Explanation: Paul says that as the Philippians learn to be humble like Christ in a world that is selfish, they need to hold firmly to the word of life. The word of life is the message about Christ and what He has done for us. The word of life is that song about Christ we studied earlier, the message about how Jesus is God who became a man, became a servant, died for our sins, and rose from the dead. Paul says that's the message we need to hold to tightly.

It's like the mountain climber reaching up and gripping the rope. He's trusting that rope to be strong enough to catch him if he falls. He's holding on tight because he knows the rope is saving him. Everyone around him can see how much he trusts the rope. That's the way we need to cling to the message about Jesus: we need to trust it, keep it in front of our faces, cling to it, and remind ourselves every day about it.

When we remember the message of life, it motivates us to be humble like Christ. When we cling to the true message God has given us in the Bible, we know that God really will give favor to the humble, just like He did Christ. We know that every time we mess up and are selfish, God will be gracious and forgive us. No matter how much we mess up, the word of life is there to tell us, "Keep going! It is worth it! And God will be there with you all the way!"

Questions for Your Kids:

1. If someone read this passage and asked you, "What is the word of life? What does that mean?" how would you answer that? (*The word of life is the message of eternal life promised in the gospel. The word of life is the message about Jesus and what He has done for us.*)

2. What is one way you can hold on to that message every day? (*Read the Bible. Pray to God. Talk to others about it. Sing songs about Jesus.*)

> **Prayer:** Pray that God will always help you remember how amazing and important the word of life is. Ask God to help you to remind each other every day about the great message of life and how it motivates us to be humble like Christ.

THE HEART OF HUMILITY
Teaching your children to put others first.

LESSON 28:
Motivation for Humility: The Day of Christ

Opening Thought:

A lot of people go away to school when they get older, and they spend years studying to get a special degree. Sometimes people might wonder why they're taking so many classes. They might say, "Why isn't he having fun? Why is she spending time reading and learning? That doesn't look like any fun. What a waste of time!" But then the last day of class comes. They take the final test, they graduate, and then they get hired by a company and start making money. Then all their friends around realize all that hard work is paying off.

Today we're going to read about the day when all our hard work obeying Christ will finally pay off.

Scripture Reading: **Read Philippians 2:14-18.**

Explanation: Remember Paul's situation as he writes this letter. He is sitting in jail, waiting for the day he would go on trial. He knew some day he could be killed for his faith in Jesus. Can you imagine what the people in Philippi were thinking about the Christians there? They were probably saying, "Why are you still following Paul? He's wasting his life. He was arrested when he was here in Philippi, and he's been arrested again. Do you want to end up like Paul? He's a complete failure."

And Paul is saying to the church in Philippi, "Remember, even if I die, that is not the end of the story. The Day of Christ is coming. That's the day that Jesus finally returns to earth, and He judges the whole world. He will reward those who served Him. If you continue to obey Christ, if you continue to become more like Christ, my ministry will have been a success. Jesus will look at me and say, 'Paul, these are the people you preached to, and see how they love me and obey me. Well done, Paul.'"

Paul is reminding them that no matter how hard life gets, no matter how much people don't like them, no matter how hard it is to obey God and be humble like Christ, look forward to the reward on the Day of Christ. Look forward to the day you will see Jesus face to face and He will say, "Well done."

Questions for Your Kids:

1. Do you think it would be easier to work hard in school if you always remembered that there was a great reward at the end? (*Yes. When we forget the reward, the work becomes even harder.*)

2. Do you think it was easier for Paul to be in prison and suffer for Christ when he thought about the Day of Christ? (*Yes. Knowing God would reward him for his hard work and suffering made all the suffering worth it.*)

3. Are there times when it feels hard to be humble? (*Yes. There are times when we really want to do something or have something, but we should more concerned about the interests of others. This requires us not to be selfish, and that can be be hard.*)

4. How can thinking about the Day of Christ help us to be more humble? (*When we think about the reward Christ will give to those who humbly served others, we are motivated to be more humble. If we think about the reward, this motivates us to serve others more.*)

> **Prayer:** Ask God to teach your family more about the Day of Christ, so you can be even more excited about that Day. Pray that God will help your family to serve others more, knowing God always sees it and He will remember to reward us on the Day of Christ.

THE HEART OF HUMILITY
Teaching your children to put others first.

LESSON 29: Motivation for Humility: The Example of Our Teachers

Opening Thought:

Have you ever heard of a "drink offering"? (*See if your children have ever heard of it. Ask them if they know about it.*)

In the Old Testament, when you wanted to bring an animal to sacrifice in the temple, you could also bring a drink offering. A drink offering was wine you would bring with you that would be poured out next to the animal as it burned on the altar. It was an extra sacrifice you gave to God, a way to tell God how much you loved Him.

In today's passage, Paul is going to talk about drink offerings.

Scripture Reading: Read Philippians 2:14-18 and Romans 12:1-2

Explanation: In the New Testament, we aren't asked to make animal sacrifices anymore. We don't need to do that. Jesus was the perfect sacrifice for our sins. No other sacrifice is needed to forgive us for our sins.

But we are asked to make sacrifices of a different kind. Unlike the dead animal sacrifices on the altar, God wants us to be *living* sacrifices. We are to live lives of true faith in Jesus. This is what pleases God. This is our gift to God.

Paul's great sacrifices to God were all the people who had faith in Jesus because of his work teaching others the gospel. Thousands of people heard about Jesus through Paul's preaching and teaching. Many people became Christians. Paul's sacrifice to God was all the churches he started, all over the world. The Philippians reading this letter were some of Paul's sacrifices or gifts to God.

Paul also says his suffering was like his drink offering to God. He was in prison for his faith. Some day he would die for his faith. He was happy to pour out his whole life to God as a gift, even if it meant suffering or death. He was joyful over the idea that he could give all of his life to Christ who had given all of Himself when he died on the cross.

Paul was setting an example for the Philippians. He was telling them to be humble, to set aside their differences and serve each other. Paul was willing to give up his whole life to serve the Philippians and other Christians. We should be willing to serve each other just like Paul did.

Questions for Your Kids:

1. Can you think of some of the great sacrifices Paul made in his life and the suffering he went through? (*See if you kids can remember any stories. If you want, read 2 Corinthians 11:24-27 where Paul lists some of the things he went through.*)

2. Did Paul have to be humble to go through all of that? (*Yes. Humility is being willing to set aside your own desires to serve others. Paul gave up his whole life to tell others about Jesus, even when it was very uncomfortable.*)

3. When you are humble and serve others more, do you think this would make you bored or sad? (*For Paul, he said it made him joyful. He was joyful that he could suffer for Christ, and he wanted the Philippians to be joyful too. Being humble doesn't mean being sad; it means finding joy in serving others.*)

> **Prayer:** Ask God to make you joyful when it comes to serving others, even if it is hard to do. Pray that God will be pleased with our sacrifice of faith and serving others.

THE HEART OF HUMILITY
Teaching your children to put others first.

LESSON 30: Review: 7 More Motivations for Humility

Opening Thought:

We've been looking very closely at this letter written by Paul to the Philippians, and the whole time he's been writing about humility. What is humility? (*Humility is thinking less about your desires and more about the interests of others. It's about remembering that we're God's creatures. We are not the center of the world; God is. We are here to serve God and others, not ourselves.*)

What is great about God is He doesn't just tell us to be humble. He gives us the motivation to be humble. He tells us *why* we should do it. Over the last several lessons, we've talked about seven different reasons. Let's read and hear them again.

Scripture Reading: Read Philippians 2:12-18

Explanation: If God had given us only one reason to be humble, it would be enough for us. But here He gives us seven.

1. Because God has saved us from the power of sin in our hearts, so we already have the desire to be obey God by being humble.
2. Because the all-powerful Spirit of God is still working inside us, making us into humble servants like Christ.
3. Because God is our Father and is pleased with us when we obey Him, so we can be glad knowing He is pleased with our humility.
4. Because the surrounding world needs to see that Christians are different, so we should be humble like Christ so they will realize Christ is real in our lives.
5. Because God has given us His word or message of life about what Christ has done for us, so we should not give up or get discouraged when we are sinful or selfish.
6. Because the Day of Christ is coming when He will reward those who were faithful to Him, so we should be humble servants looking forward to His reward.
7. Because God has given us great examples of men like Paul who gave their whole life to serve others, so we should be inspired to want to serve others the way they did.

As we go through our day, instead of just telling ourselves to be humble or to be a servant, we should think about these reasons. Think about God saving you from your sin and selfishness. Think about Him still working in your heart right now to make you more like His Son. Think about the smile on His face when you obey Him. Think about how your humility is a witness to the world about Jesus. Think about the hope you have as you read the word of life in the Bible. Think about the day Jesus comes back to give you your reward. Think about the example of humble men like Paul.

If you do this throughout the day, you will find yourself becoming more and more like Jesus.

Questions for Your Kids:

1. Which motivation to be humble is your favorite? Is there one of them that really stands out to you? (*See if one of them really catches your children's attention. Ask them why?*)

2. What are some ways you can remember that reason to be humble? (*Memorize this passage of Scripture. Pray to God, asking Him to help you remember it. Ask others to remind you about it.*)

> **Prayer:** Ask God to remind your family every day about these motivations. Pray that God will work more in your hearts to make you more like Christ, the ultimate example of humility.

ACKNOWLEDGEMENTS

I am indebted to the work of skilled Bible teachers who have explained the word of God through their speaking and writing. In particular, I thank John Piper, J. Ligon Duncan, Gordon Fee, Steven Cole, David Legge, Vincent Cheung, Alan Carr, Keith Krell, and Dale Whitehead.

Thank you to my wife Trisha for encouraging me to write this study for other families. Thank you for prompting me to use my gifts more for the kingdom of God.

Thank you to my kids for being my Bible study guinea pigs. You are on the front of my mind with every lesson I write. It's an honor to be your dad.

Made in the USA
Coppell, TX
07 September 2021